SENSE ME

Annum Salman

authorHOUSE®

AuthorHouse™ UK
1663 Liberty Drive
Bloomington, IN 47403 USA
www.authorhouse.co.uk
Phone: 0800.197.4150

Published by AuthorHouse 01/10/2019

ISBN: 978-1-7283-8312-5 (sc)
ISBN: 978-1-7283-8313-2 (hc)
ISBN: 978-1-7283-8327-9 (e)

Print information available on the last page.

Any people depicted in stock imagery provided by Getty Images are models, and such images are being used for illustrative purposes only.
Certain stock imagery © Getty Images.

This book is printed on acid-free paper.

For Mumma and Pappa, who are the reason this book exists today. Thank you for teaching me to be a fighter.

Dear reader,

As you embark on this journey, remember to allow yourself
to feel. You're strong, alive, and here with me. I hope you find
a bit of yourself in the words that I've penned through my
teenage and adult years, that you can lose yourself within. Cry,
experience, love, and come back stronger and happier.

Sense Me with all of you.

Contents

Chinese Whispers

I told them about being depressed
Holding a basket with too many eggs.
I told mother I couldn't sleep,
Told my sister, I couldn't eat.
Complained that I couldn't laugh
At the joke my father made.
But disbelief is the only thing certain
That runs in our family,
Who chose to Chinese whisper my problems
And announce loudly
That, of course,
She's happy.

Dear Mother

You never taught me how downright dirty I was just because I was born a
Girl.
You didn't teach me that being born with a vagina came with a price;
That my breasts were objects for men's eyes
And my body a museum open for visitors even if I didn't like it.
Mother, you never told me
I'd have to bite my tongue because I have no voice,
That killing me would be an honour and our country would rejoice
If I was gone;
If I ever had the courage to make my own choice.
Mother, you gave me a different name but didn't tell me I had to be the same
As everyone else,
Because being different is a crime.
Mother, if I had a dime for every time a man looked at me
And thought of how I would taste before he heard what I had to say,
We'd be rich.
Mother, you're the only one who forgot to tell me I was a mistake,
But the world doesn't let me forget.

The Narrow Escape of an Artist

I experience death every time I create art.
Moments between pits of despair, mourning, and anguish.
I grasp for air with the holding of a pen,
Scribbling words hanging like oxygen masks.
The flight can take off to heaven any minute.
You ask me how I produce my art.
Tracing over my words, you say it's magic
And indeed it is.
Reassembling broken pieces
To make myself breathe life into something else.

When Nature Roars, May I Go Outdoors?

They called him her rainbow, said he lit up the room with his colours.
Whenever he was around her,
She sparkled in all the new shades he brought to her.
But only she knew
About the storm before he appeared -
The thunder that never escaped
A closed door.

Faith

Grandeur was how I would describe you because God had excessively spent all the good on you and left less for the world. I looked at you with awe and wondered if I could convert to a religion that allowed me to worship you, whether people would finally believe I'm religious? I thought of you more than five times a day, recited your name to fall asleep, and saw you when I closed my eyes.

They say God lives in your heart but all I find inside is you. You've left no space for the divine. How am I not supposed to be obsessed with you?

Beauty And The Beast

I told him today
That I've been explored,
Like the cave that held the treasure chest of gold
That was meant to be kept closed,
Like words too taboo to be spoken.
I held the cigarette between my lips and blew,
Hoping the smoke could teach him a thing or two
Of how my tongue had been used.
I told him today,
About when the beauty met the beast
And how grand the feast
Had been -
Of what it tasted like,
Bitter and sweet,
The hunger being fed by love
And the dread
Left by those who can now never leave.
I told him today
How I've been shared
By mouths who no longer speak to me,
And I wonder if he will still
Ask me for dinner tonight.

The Elephant In The Room

When I was a child, you took me to the circus,
Where we saw acts that awed me.
I asked you ridiculous questions on the way back,
And you answered them all.
I remember us coming home on our own,
But years later, you love to bring the elephant we saw to every room I sit in.
He trumpets and doesn't let me speak,
Threatens to step over me if I try.
You ask over and over again what changed between us,
Why I don't visit enough.
I want to say,
"Your choice, your lies, my age,
Another woman, not my mother."
But your pet squeezes into the tiniest spaces
Tagging along to family events,
And when you look around you feel fulfilled.
You cannot see the emptiness
Behind the giant you carry.
Whenever people ask how we are,
You reply, "*Alhamdullilah*, we have it all,"
And I shrink my presence,
Till you notice my absence and repeat,
Tell me if something is wrong.

Accents

You laugh at my accent,
You imitate it,
I try to copy yours,
Roll my tongue to find pure white words,
Mouth-wash with superiority and correctness
So, I can pronounce properly a language learned years
Which still intimidates me to my core.
But do you have a way of saying 'you' politely, rudely or friendly?
Aap, tu, tum.
Do you have a word to describe the light on his face
Of warmth and kindness,
Nur,
Do you have a word for the feeling you feel when you cannot say no
To those you love or respect,
Takkaluf,
I learn from you, ways to blend,
Learn from me, to accept
Flaws and the spice I add,
To your street markets
And corner food shops.
And if one day you can,
InshAllah,
You too will be known for your hospitality.

Home

I ran home
On a cold night,
Where echoes of our laughter
Could ignite
A fire to keep me warm.
Home knew me well,
From the scribbles of our names
That we had left.
Home was sheltered,
He had doors of steel
And windows unshattered.
He made me feel
Everything that numbness had deprived me of.
I ran home,
Where stories untold
Would fold
With hearts poured out,
Redder than wine.
Our glasses clinked
And he was divine,
Knowing me better than the gods.
He read the lines of me like a book
I didn't know had been written,
Like a fate I had to journey towards.
He erased a past,
And we watched the future
Unfold in front of us
As we sat in the front seat.

My heart could no longer beat
As it lay bare in his palm.
He delicately pressed a finger on it -
It hurt.
He knew, and he laid a finger on it again -
It hurt.
He knew, and he laid a finger on it again -
It hurt!

Home was bitter.
He had seen me age,
Grow from a caterpillar into a butterfly.
Except I was the caterpillar who could fly,
And now I was caged,
Surrounded by pillows that smelled the same
And whips that beat me to tame
Fantasies I had learned to dream.
"You are a woman and you just sleep.
Eyes closed; hush! You do not speak."

Home was claustrophobic.
Hands around a neck.
It was sexy, and remember, you liked it?
Home had walls
Sounds could not get out of,
Like cones placed on roads.
Home was where I could not drive out from

Even with lights on,
The neighbours would not see
The suffering of the Christmas tree
As it twinkled with ornaments.
How could anyone think
Of it being ripped away from its roots
To stand at your patio?
"Beautiful", people said
Of something which was dead.

Home knew how to play the game
Of making me feel ashamed
For sins I had not committed.
Home wanted a fling.
Knowing I only knew how to love,
He played music and made me sing.
Home welcomed me with open doors and a clean mat.
I wiped off the dirt and stepped in.
Home brushed everything off
Inside,
Piling back on me what I had left behind.

Home knew where the scars were,
But it prepared a meal
With candlelit dinners
And a red dress.
Swings in the playground,
And I couldn't regress.
I ran home
Like a child who had lost his way.
I was told that strangers betray,

But friends who became foes
Are like people you do not know:
Strangers, all the same

I ran home,
But it had been destroyed by a thunderstorm.
Although it was made out of bricks,
Some disasters are strong enough
To take with them everything you had loved.
And you can cry on the grave
For you knew what was once inside.
But some marks are better left as stains
You can never get rid of.
And while they sting,
They can never bring
Memories back to life.

I ran home
To understand why I ran away.

You Are Loved

"You are loved."
I will write this on a notebook in ink
And hope you fall asleep on an open page.
Have the words sink as they imprint
Onto your face,
So every time you see your reflection
You can know
Somebody loves you.
You're never alone.

Six Feet Under

You enclosed your heart in a casket and dug a grave to place it in. It hurt too much to keep it. You lied when people asked who died. You said, "Her," but you actually meant to say, "Me." You never wrote on a tombstone, but you remember the colour of the pebbles near where it resides. They shine. You're afraid to walk by it; you tell horror stories of how you hear voices calling out to you. You don't tell anyone that they're laughs, giggling screams, soft whispers, and seducing moans.

I'm still beating to your name, dancing within this organ. You ran away, but you never turned the music off.

Anna

Anna, as a child you coloured a circle your mother had drawn on a piece of paper with blue, yellow, orange and red.
Do you remember saying that it was Earth?

Anna, you were taught about borders for the first time
When your father had to borrow money to transfer to his account to show as funds,
So you could claim to be successful just because you were in another country.
You marked on a map: rich and poor.
You knew where you wanted to be.

Anna, you speak the language of those who had conquered your land before you had been born.
Today, you can write an essay on the effects of colonization in words that aren't even your own

Anna, you came packaged, labelled, stereotyped like stamps of religion injected onto newborn bums.
Will you ever be able to forget how you felt being interrogated by an immigration officer at the airport?

Anna, you wonder how you can still sound different when you have soaked and baptised yourself in the history of your rulers.
You remain an import, brought in to learn more from those certified with knowledge to impart.

Anna, you often forget the difference between you and your friends until you have a form to fill in, with ten extra questions specific to you.

Why do you try so hard to blend in, when the system has been designed to divide?

Anna, you are constantly rejecting the idea of home and place of birth being one.

Is it out of hope that some place will call you their own out of sympathy?

Anna, your identity feels like a phantom limb.

It suddenly appears when you're at a dinner and can swallow down spicy food like a bad ass,

Without dashing for a glass of water.

Doesn't it always feel like a revelation that you still possess what you inherited, even after wanting to get rid of it?

Anna, you feel privileged when they ask you where you're from. You take pleasure from knowing it's because you're fair.

Can you remember how it felt to not feel intimidated just by a look?

You were taught that staring is impolite, but apparently it's only a rule for a brown person.

Anna, you have started to walk with hunched shoulders. The weight of your nation's reputation lies on you as a responsibility.

Have you tried climbing into another skin and imitating them so well that little girls no longer holler, "Solar eclipse!" When you walk into the day?

Anna, you have been a bird in flight for years,

Not allowed to settle down because your wings are too bright for some.

You always wanted to be the centre of attention,

But now you hate standing out,

Because being different means you have to carry a shield to protect yourself from the bullies.

You thought school was over,

But life is a new battlefield where the bell never rings to call it quits.

Anna, you did not just opt for ease; you chose to stop resonating to images of terrorists, just by the sound of your name
Now it feels like a cactus, stuck in your throat when you try to spit it out,
Knowing it will poke you anyway when somebody else asks you to spell it out.
You'll spell out, "E-M-B-A-R-R-A-S-S-M-E-N-T."
Embarrassment!
Isn't it funny that somebody else's mispronunciation makes you feel small?

Anna, nobody will understand the art of camouflage as well as you do.
You can't even see yourself in your own reflection anymore.

Anna, when your mother and grandmother call,
You lower your voice and comfortably speak,
Leaving your disguise behind. For a moment, you're unafraid of saying something wrong.
And maybe home is forgiveness
For being allowed to be ourselves.
Maybe home is where you're called by your name.

Anna, will you miss being called Annum?

One Minus One Equals Zero

The night refuses to show me my shadow.
The world is too afraid to see what I've become without you.

Night-Time

I was afraid of change. Your being around created differences only my eyes could see. It was like the realities were chameleons that would blend and disappear when anybody else looked, and we talked about dreams only we knew existed. You've woken me up from my sleep; I now stay awake, suffering from insomnia, sharing visions with imaginary friends. You knew I was afraid of change, and you'd become routine. I now live in fear of never returning to my fantasy.

Hang Your Vocabulary

If my body is a closet, my tongue is the skeleton that rattles with all the dead wishes I made, and the rotten words I never said.

The Last Dance

Tap, tap, tap
Will you join the lovers
That reunite
When the flowers die,
And the clouds blow away to expose a sky,
Full of dead stars that don't shine?

Tap, tap, tap.
Will you step onto the dance floor,
Rock your soul, hum to the music and help it remind you
Of the heartbeat you used to have?

Tap, tap, tap.
Can you name all the monsters dancing
Once they are out from under the bed?
Can you describe their faces,
Or do you only know what they feel like
when they breathe down your neck?

Tap, tap, tap.
Can you force a smile when it's all too real?
When everyone is invited to your home for a party
And you aren't even a host,
Will you confess that you lost the invites?
That you thought of them but didn't mean to call everyone,
Because you weren't ready?
But nobody is allowed to take their time and space.

Tap, tap, tap.
The last song that plays.
You want them to play it at your funeral,
When your anxiety, depression and
loneliness are sitting in the front row,
Giving speeches of their memories with you,
When they are alive and you are not.

Tap, tap, tap.
You will still hear the heels knocking against your grave
Of those you left behind.
Because expressing yourself meant defeat,
Exposed feelings hurt less than death.
Your secrets remain
And will entertain
Guests to keep questioning.

My Body

I am broken down by my consciousness,
When you hold me.
I wish the heat between us could shrink.
You could arrange my body
So it fits perfectly with yours.

•

My body is innocent,
Treated with love.
It swells with happiness,
But your touch makes me want to
Push my fingers down my throat.
So, you can feel a hollow tummy,
That rumbles of not enough,
But creates a space for your words to echo
"You're beautiful."

•

My body thinks I'm a hypocrite.
I speak about eating well,
But I don't want to embrace my own advice,
All my body does is listen,
And all I do is punish it
By shaming it
For being itself.

The Galaxy

Your body lies close, your back turned towards me. While the sun shines from the window, illuminating your silhouette, you sleep absolutely. The gaps between your backbones map out a trail for my fingers to trace over, from the bottom of your spine to the crown of your neck. I spot the marks on your body and draw out figures like constellations in the sky. Needless to say that I don't need a shooting star to pass by to make a wish upon. If you stay, I will live here for eternity, bowed down on the smell of your skin, like a pilgrim kissing the holy wall he wants to be blessed by. I will live here, lost in admiration of your grace. Mute in your company, not because I have nothing to say, but because words compete in my throat to come out first. I hope they can form a sentence to praise you in the way you deserve.

An Apology

When I was born,
My mother whispered, "Sorry" into my ear instead of a prayer.
It stuck to my tongue like a catchphrase
That I could gift wrap and present
As a penance for mistakes I was never sure I made.
Like my sorry was charity for the underprivileged
And I was rich with apologies.
I distributed sorry like candy on Halloween.
Whether you asked for it or not,
The lights at my home were always on for you
To come and see me, down on my knees,
Ready to please
You.

"I'm sorry", I said.
When he told me he had fallen out of love with me,
I did not know where to carve another hole.
Since I had already given him my heart,
I pushed my hand down my throat, trying to find another organ
He could find space in.
And when he made excuses of the winter being too harsh,
Wanting to leave,
I said, "Sorry", because God did not always listen to me.
But the cave he had carved in me
Was for him to hibernate in.

He had to go, so I said, "Sorry".
Knowing my body was never warm enough,
I started to rub my skin against wood,
Hoping it would catch fire,
So he could find me habitable.

"I'm sorry", I said.
Every time he yelled,
His voice ringing like church bells
Loud enough to wake the dead from their graves.
I wanted to hush him down
As I lay broken on the ground
Like confetti at a party
I did not want to be a host of.
My sorrys were like lullabies;
If I could sing them for long enough,
Maybe I could put his anger to sleep.

When none of it worked,
I still said, "Sorry", for trying so hard,
For having too many feelings.
He'd call me over-emotional,
Like being sensitive was a disease.

But some habits are hard to get rid of,
Like blood stains on bed sheets.
My aunt told me,
When her husband lay her on the bed at the age of sixteen
And she consciously covered her breasts,
She murmured, "Sorry",
For being herself.
My friend tells me
The Day of Judgment is definitely near.
She has already lived hell on earth
In the house of her in-laws,
Where she dresses up the dining table with food
And throws sorry on the table as bait,
To help her cooking taste good enough, hot enough, spicy enough,

As she swallows her pride
For being the bride
Of a man she has chosen to love.

Sorry has been sewn into my flesh and bones.
Sealing lips that can't express
Anything, other than the need for mercy.
For I can't walk into a room anymore
Without greeting the audience with "Sorry".
If only my presence would get the attention it deserves!
I grew up this way,
Wishing for hands like an octopus,
So I can keep giving and never receiving.

But I did not understand
That my mother did not whisper, "Sorry"
To prepare me for the worst,
But as a plea of forgiveness,
For bringing me into a world
That was going to teach me how to speak,
And then take away my voice.

When the Iron Meets a Cloth

He became her panacea.
Like heat can straighten out the creases of a crumpled paper,
His warm body
Could smooth out
The lines on her forehead.

Obituary

You were a star. No, you were the damned sun. Dancing in the middle of the room, admirers orbited you. But you twisted your ankle and cried, exaggerating your pain. You made excuses bigger than they were. You became a black hole, refusing to illuminate any darkness. Your humour called millions to see your show, but the performer at the circus had blown himself up, taking with him 500 casualties who died smiling. You're famous today. Existing in black and white, you're documented in a file, not the way you wanted to be remembered. Fame and insanity are two different lines. Why did you never look down to see which one you had jumped upon?

My Ex Called

I thought I had lost you. I wasn't upset about it. Yes, I was finally alone and it felt awkward, like the sensation of a phantom limb. I'd shudder at the thought of you, breathe and wonder if you were still there because of how used to you I was. But my heart was beating fine; no palpitations like a child playing hopscotch. I was finally sober. I'd walk in a straight line without thinking.

Maybe you thought I rang, because you gave me a wakeup call the other day. Just because I think of you, does not mean I want you back. You're latching on again, like I slept in a dirty place and picked you up like a disease, although nobody agrees that you are to be treated like an illness. No matter how hard I try to explain how toxic this relationship is, you're given the benefit of the doubt of not existing. I know that empowers you, so you come back, because who will believe that we're together? Who lets what destroys them back into their life, right? What conversations should I stop having that bring you closer, when my energy vampire lives within me? You've become a feared joke, making me the punch line.

Knock, knock.

I don't want to ask who's there; anxiety.

I'm not opening this door.

Wonder Woman

I was asked to remain silent when confronted with the face of anger. When my fingers would begin to curl up into an iron fist, an emerging scowl would become prominent; a hush would slow me down. It was like turning off the kettle. A blink of caring eyes, soothing me, reminding me of how short a moment is.

Breathe, let it pass, be the bigger person.

Oh Mother, how expanded is your heart by the hurt you've digested, the insults you've swallowed and the scabs never given time to heal? How do you remove arrows and not throw them back to prove a point? How do you keep looking so soft when the world has made you metal from the inside? How are you so strong, yet so kind?

The Only Fish in her Ocean

She was a walking tissue box
Who'd peel off her skin
To wipe away your tears.
So, you started to call her misery.
When you shed water over her shoulders,
She soaked everything in,
Like your grief was her oxygen.
She radiated her light in return.
You were alive
And she was drowning.
But she was okay with it.

I Took the Best of You With me; You'll Find Your Complete Self in my Memories.

If you take out the gold
From a treasure chest,
Would anybody want to go on a hunt to find it?

You have lost your value,
Broken boy.
You're not the same
Without your heart.

I Found Words

In third grade English class.
An empty piggy bank,
A distressed father,
A house under construction.
I found words.
The first time, my heart leapt, and I found
myself describing it as a frog.
I was a hybrid;
I found words.

To explain the shade of his brown eyes,
That the colour wheels couldn't define,
I made up mine.
I found words.

When nobody could understand what sound I was talking about,
When I told them about the crack
I had heard in my body,
It was my heart
When he stopped having anything to say.
I found words.

When the clothes stopped fitting me,
When depression was eating me,
I filled my mouth with cake.
And the only thing that could come out;
Two fingers down my throat,
Trying to lose weight,
Were words.

I found them,
When my hands could no longer find your head.
Stretched,
An empty pillow case.
I found words
When solace was no longer solitude,
When everyone's complaint was,
"What's wrong with your attitude?"
And my feelings couldn't match
My tone,
Blocked, blind and alone.
I found words

That stood around,
Twirled and danced,
Cried and laughed,
And made me whole.
I found words.

Blind to the Dark

Don't listen to him,
He who tells you you're not enough,
So you stammer when you speak
And hide,
Thinking you're a freak.
Don't listen to him,
He who tells you that
You will fail,
You are weak,
You are the boat that will sail
Through every storm.
You weren't born
To lose.
Don't listen to him,
The inner voice.
He only thinks of defeat;
He is a cheat.
A foe pretending to be friend.
Don't listen to him,
The demon inside.
Your dreams are your guide;
Listen to them.

Frame It

I'll create a painting for you,
Drawn with blood,
And hope that my art can convey my hate to you
Through the colour of love.

Hate: A Love Story

You can choke on your sleep
With a cactus deep in your throat.
You shouldn't have loved a writer.

Bitterness stings
Like an aftertaste of ink.
You shouldn't have loved a writer.

She stole your words for show and tell,
Dissecting ribs of the skeleton in your closet.
You shouldn't have loved a writer.

She'll story-tell your flaws,
You'll feel your tongue writhe in pain.
You shouldn't have loved a writer.

She'll make you vomit your breakup,
Readers will scream at the last cliff-hanger.
You shouldn't have loved a writer.

She'll autograph her bestseller in your name,
Make you savour the sourness of hate.
Oh, you shouldn't have loved a writer.

Strangers That Smell Like Home

I find home in the conversations with the man who drives a cab.
He doesn't know me,
But has a lot of concern that I live here without family.
He tells me about his daughter -
"She's doing a Master's like you. I'm proud of her."
- And charges me less for the ride.
I remember him,
And he says he'll remember me.
He accepted the ride because I sounded Muslim anyway.
I laugh at the bigotry,
But accept his gesture to make me feel welcomed
In a place of anonymity.

I like going to the shop five miles from my house,
More than the corner one.
They sell the same products,
But the lady who packs my bags
Knows secrets I don't tell anyone,
And she whispers sweet words in the language of nostalgia.
She knows it brings me more comfort than dread.

I take friends to taste the kind of food that will make them turn red,
But every bite is cooked with love,
And I scoop so much of it on my plate,
That I don't leave any white spots.
For the first time, they say, "That was fast,"
As I swallow and let the spices warm me up like the summer of Karachi.
For once I am hot, and unwrap the scarf and the coat that envelops me.
I scan customers as I work at the McDonald's till,
And I find your worrying eyes.
You have a loose *dupatta* covering your head,
And your nervous fingers look like they're knitting an invisible sweater.
I call for you.
You make your way with steady steps and try to pronounce what you'd like.
I let you take your time,
Watch you struggle,
And choke on words that deceive you every time.
You're like a child,
Mumbling, stumbling, having somebody else correct you.
I know your order every time.

Halfway through it, I speak in our tongue,
And your eyes spark with delight.
The sound of familiarity is music,
A kind voice that gives you the choice
To be at ease.
You bless me as you leave,
And I can see it float in the air,
Following me while I walk home,
Protecting me as I sleep.

The angels I look for these days
Understand the anguish
Of rubbing their skins
And spitting their accents
To no avail,
Other than to accept that wherever home may be,
No matter how hostile
The city,
There will always be neighbours who have sugar.

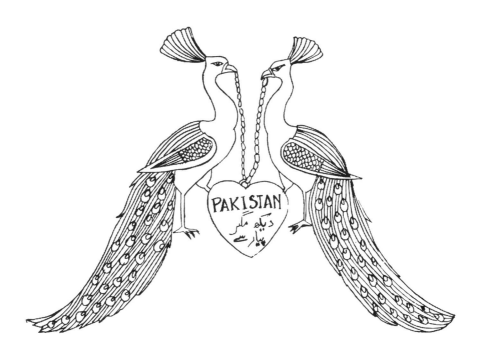

A Trick Question

I find nothing of you
In any other man I meet,
And I'm not sure
Why I look for a broken man
In someone complete.

Average

It's tormenting
To take off clothes
And never be able to change
Out of this skin.
I'm willing to walk in the shoes
Of someone else.
I refuse this abuse
Of living with myself.
Erase my name
And train my body
Not to exist.
Pull off the nice eyes
And the red lips.
Naked, we'll celebrate
The demise
Of the ordinary.

Diary With a Lock

Mother, I can't let you read the words I write,
For you may think I'm a liar.
I'm being burnt by a fire
You cannot see,

Fighting a war
You cannot free
Me from.

Mother, I want you to believe
That I carry my heart on my sleeve,
Because I don't have another explanation for these scars I write about.
I don't want you to doubt
My happiness.

Mother, it is true what the words say,
Much to your dismay.
But nothing is your fault;

You loved me right.
It's just that the demons fight
Me more than others.

Mother, you keep the lights on,
Since you discovered I write in the dark.
Avoiding nightmares, I stay awake,
But even sunshine cannot shake
Away my fear.
Oh Mother dear,
You cannot help me.

These words I ink
Will sink
Me under another world,

Better than here.

When Age is a Large Number

Her delicate hands now feel fragile,
Decorated with veins,
A hunch in her back,
And an ache in her knee.
Every time, I visit home,
The walls of your house has more cracks,
The doors creak more,
Meals are cooked lesser,
Discussions are more about fatigue,
You repeat, over and over and over again,
How you need to keep seeing me more,
And I'm afraid that the next time we meet,
You won't recognize me anymore.
We wish you on your birthday,
Debate about how old you are,
Checking old photo albums with their dates,
And finding ID cards you have replaced,
With newer ones.
Your skin droops, your hair fall,
Time is running,
But our conversations are slow,
As you forget how many teaspoons of sugar you've put in your tea,
I respond to my sister's name,
When you tell me how much you love me.

No Voice

You tell me I can say no if I don't want to do something,
And I nod my head to your words,
Because I was never taught to disagree.
Even if I wanted to, I wouldn't know how.
You see, I've been taught to appease
And use words that only please men.

"Yes," has been the ancestral gem passed down as an inheritance
From Grandma, to Ma. We all wore it like a crown,
So nobody ever asks for my opinion when even the blind
Sense my consent.

Family Secret

You are a broken plate,
Smashed at the dinner table.
A Ruined evening,
The sounds of gasps and hushes.
No pile of bones,
But a grave has been dug
To bury our silences in.
Nobody will talk about your depression;
You will continue
Living it.

Brown

I'm so white-washed
That brown is foreign,
Even to me.
Urdu does not roll easily,
Sweat gathers on the top of my forehead
When I need to speak,
And I'm afraid my pronunciations will reveal
That I'm not ready to be
Desi.
I flaunt English words,
Like they were written down in scripts,
Revealed to me generations before
I could say
My very first words.
Now I can speak fluently
In a language
Not understood by my mother,
And proudly
Claim as I hold a passport green,
I'm Pakistani.

Change

I'm thinking of a way
To grow out of you,
Like you're a shirt
I wore in my childhood.
I can keep it as a memory,
It could still smell the same,
But it cannot fit me anymore.

The Angry Nobody

My mother asks why I'm so angry. When she celebrates my birthday and counts the candles on the cake, her smile is fake and concerning.
The shining flame reflects the tears in her eyes and I'm afraid that I bring her shame.
What have I done, to have grown from a womb and lived in a house she made me call home
For longer than I belonged?
Every cake I blow on feels like a murder of a desire she holds for me; to walk on the stage
In a red bridal dress, handing me to a man I don't know the name of yet, like the baton in a relay race.
"There you go, it's your turn now stranger" to hold her and run, we are done.
She has been done since I turned eighteen.

My father asks why I'm so angry.
As we sit down to dinner, he fills his plate with food without a concern as to whether there would be enough left for anybody else.
I do not blame him; the man was brought to earth as a whole
And always needs to be full,
Unlike the women in my family, who were taught that emptiness will always be rewarded.
You see, looking at the glass as half full has been our bible.
We were taught to see and not touch, and wished that it applied to men when we stepped out of our homes,
But our fathers and brothers have never experienced hunger.
Their cravings have always been satisfied, so no matter how full they are after lunch or dinner, they're always looking for dessert,

And everything tastes like a meal.

My father asks why I'm so angry, as he gives the women in the house a look if we fill up our plates with as much food as his.

My boyfriend asks why I'm so angry.

Every time, after we fix a fight, I realise the only word I've been saying for the past hour is "Sorry."

Those apologies have been sewn into my bones, tattooed on my body, reflected in the mirror I stand in front of.

I am always the mistake, the unthought of words said too soon,

A little too honest for your taste.

I have become desensitised to the presumptions put on me,

So my love flows naturally like a popped champagne bottle.

I can't even remember when I threw the cork away, who I threw it away for.

My body is a peace maker; I offer it as a treaty to resolve a war.

Even when he is wrong, he wins.

I have been made to believe that without him I am nobody,

Like I did not come here alone, that I will not be dug into the ground and have to live with my own silence.

A mute bed shared with him is already a grave.

When I write, when I speak, before I go to sleep,

I ask myself why I'm so angry.

Because I can be.

I owe it to my voice to demand the right of my tongue to communicate
what this heart feels,
Because change is integral to growth
And I am done being stuck in a zone where only repression thrives.
I'm angry because nobody passed me an extinguisher for the fire caused
by the injustices done to me.
I'm angry because you have let me be,
Because you've taken away from me what I deserve and made me believe
in what you think I deserve.
I am angry because I don't know who I would be
Without your expectations of me.

Zainab

Maybe you saw it on the news,
Or you read it online in this age of the social.
Nobody talks anymore, but the conversations go on,
And you can block your ear holes,
Press your palms and dig in your fingers and block out the noise,
And you will still hear an eight year old scream in pain.
Shut your eyes then,
Squeeze your eyelids and imagine the faces of the men you voted for,
And wonder whether they feel a man's hand crawling over their daughters'
bodies, and if they wake, yelling,
Banging down their bedroom doors in fear that somebody may be over
their little girls,
Forcing, taking them away from what is made to be called their homes.
And when they breathe their sigh of relief for their place is safe,
They tuck themselves in and sleep comfortably.
Do you then go out and observe
Your neighbours, the postman, the school teachers, your family friends?
Everyone wears a blindfold, like the justice system;
Imbalanced, the bad weighing it down,
Digging up the ground with guilt, shame, unfair, lazy fights never fought,
Tiny bodies not rescued but laid to their graves.
Maybe you will sleep tonight, and hug your loved ones tight,
And hope that tomorrow will be better when the sun rises to a new day,
And a new day and a new day and a new day.
Secure you, in your secure home,
It's the same day for somebody else
In a torturous home,
An innocent face hanging in a picture frame, pleading for you to save
The rest of the world.

The Inevitable

You ask me why my heart is beating so fast.
When you place your fingers on my wrist,
You say you hear a stampede.
You tell me my veins are deep blue,
That you like how you can see them prominently, lying under my skin,
And I tell you these lines represent the ocean in me,
And the thumps of my heart
Are the mermaids dancing.
You laugh, "What are mermaids doing inside you?"
Waiting.
When you leave,
I will die, cutting open the underworld that lives within me,
And my women will save me,
Gain a pair of legs,
And learn to walk with new feet,
Live like a baby,
Help me breathe.

Harassment Was a Game of Temperatures

Cold,
Caught like a book waiting to be read,
Shining on a shelf.
Cold,
Like a bet on a horse race,
Observed, desired, yet able to run away.
Warm,
Like Mum's best-cooked meal.
Uh-oh, you can only devour after guests leave.
Warm,
You're allowed to sleep over,
But rules say, lights out after eleven.
Hot,
In an elevator, the space between them.
Hot,
He squeezes into her cubicle at work.
Hot,
He pushes her into a ladies-only bathroom.
Hot,
My own doctor doesn't understand where it hurts.
Hot,
I went to school to study not…
Hot,
"Nonsense, he's blood-related."

Taste of a Familiar City

The scorching sun of Karachi burnt on her back.
The heat of the sandy beaches warmed up her heart
So when she walked in to your icy cold home,
Your fire alarm rang.
You mistook the smoke as mist,
Forgot you believed love is a myth,
And embraced her in your arms,
Melting the snow.
Summer came sooner.

Chapter Two

The salt in my tears
Will be sprinkled over your wounds.
When you see the man in my smile
Has made me reconcile
With my past,
You remain no more.

Nomad

I'm hanging in a gallery.
An artefact, post-war,
Of a huge massacre and bombs.
The hospital beds have been emptied,
The surgical instruments remain inside me.
They talk of soldiers with missing limbs;
I miss my heart.
Surviving and living are two different things.
They visit to observe my scars;
They've conquered my land,
And plan to rehabilitate.
But where do those go,
Who could never articulate
Where they belong?

A Rigged Game

Even when he reaches his hand out,
Pushes it down your throat
And pulls out your heart,
He will still tell you
How it's your fault
For not eating well enough,
Or feeling more than what was necessary.
Of how you are mistaken
For assuming your organ is strong.
And you'll lie,
Bleeding, half alive,
Consciously hating yourself
For being easy
Once again.

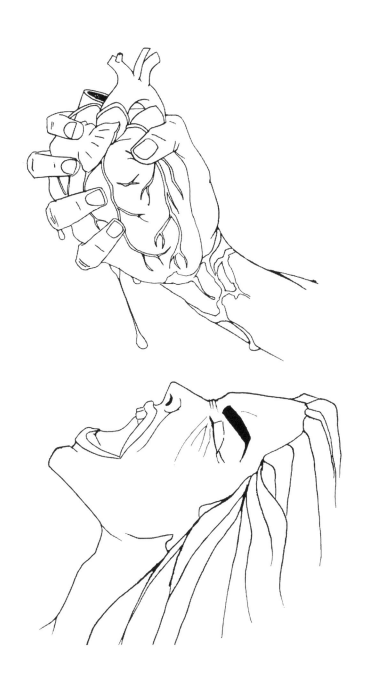

There's Always One Poem About Him

I had to pull out poems from under my skin,
To build a string of words to feel
Like a wild animal, pulling at the meat of its prey.
I could pray all night and have no letters to chew on
And vomit in spite, to create art one could remember.

Now I lay and let myself hear your heart beat, and my own dance to the
rhythm
That you are alive, and you are mine.
Now words have a destiny to fulfil,
Of being carved in your memory
Stronger than the tips of my fingers that caress your body,
Or my kisses that linger on your lips and miss you the moment you're away.
I'm a poet and a writer, half for you.
I'm a lover and a fighter, all for you.

Declare All Wounds Here

Maybe I was the customary stop for the heartbroken,
With a sign hung around my neck: "All damaged goods, deposited here."

Clean Up Before the Guests Arrive

We've burdened love to be our fixer,
Like it's the last child
And all the ones before it have failed
To satisfy us with what they could be, how they could've made us proud.
Now love, love has to be held responsible for bringing us the happiness we sought,
So we groom ourselves for it.
While we are searching,
Presenting our best foot forward,
Not knowing if a limb is being asked for,
But we're willing to sacrifice
Anything to gain that joy,
Films talk about.
Love is afraid to be found,
Because love doesn't fix;
Love only fills
Spaces that are cracked.
Love pours out and reaches places it doesn't belong,
Where it hurts.
So, we blame love for failing,
For seeping out,
Reaching the pits of us,
We had never explored.
The darkness within
Never gets lit
When the caves haven't been visited
By us.

Blank

The weight of emptiness is increasing
Day by day.
It's ironic,
How heavy something missing
Can feel.

The Career Ladder I Want You to Climb

How can I stand tall enough
To become a goal
You'd like to reach?

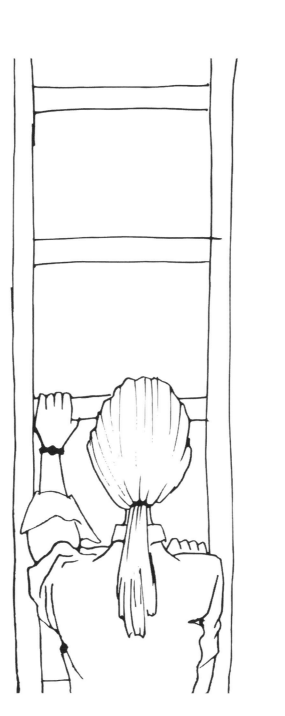

What Happened?

I heard how you want to kill yourself. I was left wondering how a cynosure could stop being the centre of everyone. Like suddenly, crowds started to gather, not to hear you laugh, but with buckets to fill your tears with, so they could water their own plants. Like you drew a ring of fire, like the fire dancers we saw on the beach when we were together, and how we sat in the distance, for fear of catching it on our skins. I wonder how your company became boring enough so your conversations became paper planes, flying overhead, your eyes glassy enough so people could only see themselves and look through you. When did you stop being loved, when that's all I had taught you?

He Stutters

I am strung together by my mistakes,
Knitted with heartbreak
And disjointed relationships
Of those who never stayed.
So, when you kiss me,
Don't be surprised
If I cut your tongue.
I was never pieced back correctly.
I apologise for the damage loving me will cause;
You will never sound the same again.

Her Tears Water Plants of Misery

Remember that when you love me, my anxiety will love you back first. When you're gone, she's wide awake. Even when I lay, she's drumming to a tune she says we played together once. I tell her she's mine, but she refuses to agree; she has made herself yours. When you're here I smile, but she's dancing on ice skates and winter is coming to an end. Oh, when you love me, remember, I bury my loss and grieve, but my anxiety roots from the graves.

You're A Queen

It's been ingrained in you,
The need for acceptance.
So, even when he yells in your face,
Screams insults and breaks every bit of self-esteem you built,
You crawl back to him.
You collect the sea to wash yourself to taste better for him,
You cook food to build a way to his heart,
You vacuum every corner of your house,
Sucking away the sins you believe you have committed,
And you kneel on your prayer mat and plead to
God to let the devil stay.
It's been ingrained in you,
To be patient with abuse and impatient for the future.
You choose the now
And call it heaven.
But weren't you told that Satan takes human form,
And does not bow to the queen?
He will bend your back and walk over you,
He will take the lead.
You can choose to dance with him,
Or to turn off the music
And call off this show.
You hold the power,
You have control.

Serve

My mother taught me
That only when I placed a tooth under my pillow, would a tooth fairy replace it
With money.

Mythological characters also loved the right way, give and take.

Where then did I learn to be
A tray of sweets at a party
For guests who refused to leave?

There wasn't a meal after dessert,
Visitors devoured and love only hurt.

How did I learn to be
Used?

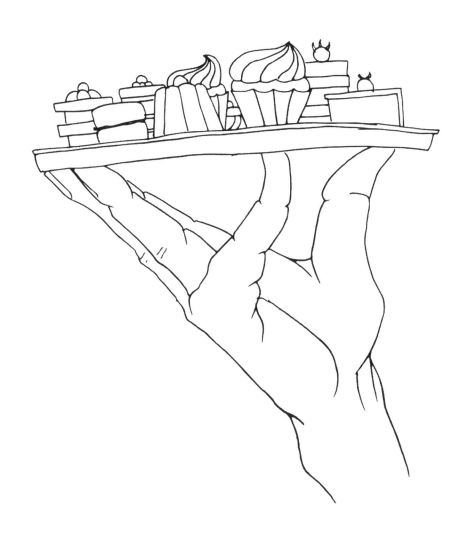

Always High Season

And I was a hotel,
Always fully booked
When he built a cave in me,
Only to never reside there.

Comfort Zone

Oh, woman who lives in a bubble,
Step out for once and see
The flowers your home rests upon.
The thorns are being held by someone else,
So you can rest in peace while their hands bleed,
Ensuring only the petals touch your feet.
Oh, woman who lives in a bubble,
It doesn't physically have to hurt to feel pain.
You are sheltered while they soak in the rain.
You say you face no discrimination, no gender inequality and the world
is so fair,
How could you dare to speak for everyone, when you cannot relate
To never having food fill up a plate?
Oh, woman who lives in a bubble of privilege,
pop it and be real.

They'll Settle on You, But
I Won't Say "Hello"

I may stay quiet at the sight of you,
But stare a little longer
And my body will break, and butterflies will escape.
No longer fighting for space in my stomach,
They'll explode freely, flying in forbidden territory.
As a child, I was able to catch them in glass jars.
As an adult, my tongue is the only thing behind bars.
I'm a prisoner of my truth,
And you, the keeper of my conservatory.

Too Real

They told you to be yourself,
So you thought,
You read,
You made art,
You spoke,
You asked
Many questions nobody could answer.
They told you to stop being like yourself.
Please, don't be yourself
At parties,
At the mosque,
At school.
You are obnoxious, you are rude,
Nobody understands the things you say.
You cause dismay,
We will ignore
The truth that comes out of you.

Lineage

I come from a generation of women who sat, cross-legged, uncomfortably.

Women who shushed each other when one of them tried to speak,
who locked their lips, tied their ankles and dropped the keys
into pockets of coats they weren't allowed to wear.

I come from the line of women who had their shoelaces tangled,
so they'd hop along like they're jumping over fire, rather than bend down,
untie the knots, and walk with ease.

I come from a line of women who would never cease
to demean themselves as just the cooks in the kitchen,
because a man demanded them to be.

I come from a line of women who went to school and were handed books
they were never allowed to read.

I come from a line of women who accepted the lesser as their fate, and to this date
their misery is blamed on their destiny.

Somewhere in a coat, rattling,
lies the key
to happiness.

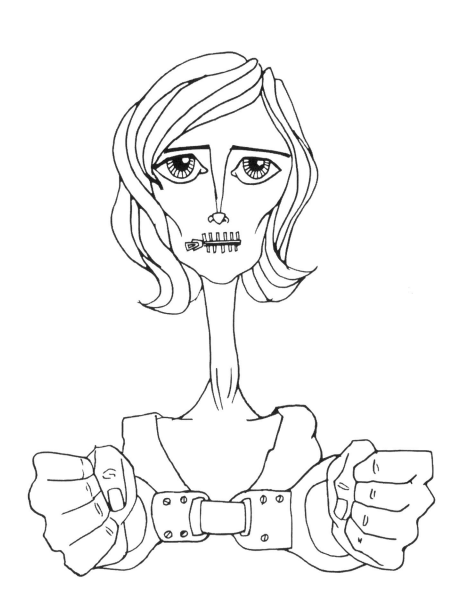

The Other Side of The Story

Maybe it wasn't love. Maybe it was the need for someone to accept parts of us we couldn't digest. Maybe it wasn't tears, but a built-up well being pulled by those who were hurt to clean their wounds. Maybe it wasn't a divorce, but a runner, quitting after losing sight of the finish line. Maybe he would have stayed if she hadn't started rooting for herself.

Unable

What if I stretched my hands up in the sky, would you have seen me then, gasping for air? I never felt the pain when you tattooed your name over my body, but now your arm chokes me at night. When you ask me to moan your name in delight, do you see the tears roll down my cheek as I scream? I never agreed, but the body language you learned taught you that a shaking woman wasn't displaying fear, but pleasure. You continued. My hands are up in the sky, but I cannot fly. With your feet strong on my cape, you continue the rape, and all I do is watch.

Not Your Punch line

I am heir of the dragon,
Evolved into a roaring lion.
When they say my name,
They spit fire.
A hot angry soul,
I cannot be caged.
I will burn the whole
Place down,
Restricted.
Before you break me down to labels, remember
I come from the lineage of the wild.
Taming words will not tame
My purpose.
I am the prisoner who will escape,
Just to put you back in your place.
I am known to the world as a woman;
Do not accept my silence as defeat.
The wise use the scarcity of words
To tiptoe through the noise.
Unnoticed, I create thunderstorms.
Can you imagine what I could do,
Free?

I Am

A pedestrian in a busy city street,
Where the rich in their long coats stride past without a second look.

I am
The fly buzzing around an ear, hoping that even if it's by annoyance,
Maybe the hand swatting me away will touch me.

I am
Homeless in a place where houses are sold,
Like the realtors can envision the number of laughs that'll roar out of the windows,
Soaring up to the sky like fireflies.

I am
A stranger, stuck between peering eyes at airports and subways.
During rush hour, busy days, a moment freezes,
Sight in slow motion, like men have drank love potions.

I am
A spare minute given to observe the untied laces on shoes,
And the dirt on the fringes at the bottom of my jeans,
Judgments solidified like I've fallen into quick sand.

I am
The artist that sits in the corner, wondering about the possibilities of the end of the world,
Because nobody has proven that breathing will increase the chances of living.
I can draw your existence on a canvas to last an eternity,

While you question the purpose of the determination
I put behind a paint brush that doesn't pay a penny.

I am
The funds you put in to feed the lies of the politicians
Who promise to build you your future, because even the blind can dream
in colour.

I am
The student at the coffee shop, soaking up wisdom like a sponge to vomit
on to an exam paper the next day,
That will define which corporation I will sell my soul to.
Some days you'll find me advertising healthcare, and other days, God.
Did you know I have the power to make you believe that the one with all
the power resides where I say he belongs?

I am
The small thing that weighs the heaviest,
Carried in your palm, holding the world at your fingertips,
Beating with beep, tweet, Instagram re-grams that beat feaster than your
heart.
I carry stories of people I've never seen,
And the friend that lies his head on your shoulder
Needs to book an appointment for you to hear his worries.

I am
The uninterested, safe and brave, just on your face; a generation
That has lost the will to look you in the eye and admit that I am lost.

I am
The tourist who pays millions to help me explore myself;
I've never been here before.

I am
Addicted to sex on screen, books and billboards that teach me violence
I cannot use to make love.

I am
Spinning like a washing machine,
Cleaning myself of the past so you can like me better.

I am
The running label of a brighter tomorrow,
With a price tag hung around my neck, pleading for you
To buy my presence in exchange for attention.

I am
Bereft of friendships and hungry in a world that throws away their food
After taking a photograph of what their plate looks like.

I am
Here today, and will be gone before you know it, with the regrets that I
lived,
Leaving nothing behind in a land to be remembered by; just remembered
While alive.

Seasons

She let parts of her shed in Autumn
Grow out of her roots.
She let the pain crawl its way out of her;
Past lovers, failed expectations, shattered dreams,
Exposed and eventually dead.
There's beauty in every flaw,
And every mistake left
An admirable spot.
The next time you meet, you'll see,
In her personality,
A bit of her from another season.

Underprivileged

Why don't you ever ask?

I was never asked. To object, to repeat, when my voice fell on deaf ears like silence. My opinions were dismissed, so I stopped giving words for free, like charity. This mouth did not open to speak but was only open at night to go down on my knees. I don't ask, because I was never asked, so I don't grieve over a plate half-full; I accept it as not empty.

Awake

I wake up at 9,
It's a normal time.
I'm happy
I didn't have nightmares.
I text and tell my friends,
It took me only two hours to fall asleep last night.
Closing my eyes has become a privilege.
I'm afraid of going back home,
Because the woman who knows every trace of my body
Will notice how my eyes have sunk,
Like they're oases in the middle of deserts.
"Why are they wet?"
She'll ask me if I'm okay.
"I am pretty fine",
It's a rehearsed line now,
Because untired faces around me are pretty damn tired of hearing the same thing.
This anxiety is bothering me.
And monotony kills relationships;
That's the reason he left.
We don't need more people to leave me at this stage,
So we'll find synonyms for 'fine'
That sound like music to people who take the word as their cue to instantly look away.
Mother, though, isn't easy to convince.
She still passes looks of doubt and says, "You ought to take care of yourself."
I tell her to shush,
"Don't let me know I need to be taken care of."
I will think of it all night; how I'm a burden on the world.
My bedroom looks great. The things are placed in order,
And it's comforting with an anxiety disorder
To know that at least some things are where they belong.
The closed walls are familiar silence -

Silence of the waiting monsters who appear after dark.
I feel like a little child.
As everybody says goodnight
And the noises die,
It starts ringing like the bell of school.
The bullies come riding through the moon,
Landing into my room
With insecurities, judgments,
The past and the future,
And death.
I am exhausted of being in this waiting room;
They keep lying about the appointment.
I'm resurrected every morning,
When the light of the sun blinds my mind.
I'm confused as to whether I'm meeting God,
Or is it again just show time?
No printed receipts of rhythm slips,
Just another trip to Hell and back.
Spent another day being a fool,
"Oh, little girl, your time ain't so soon."
This game will be played till you give up,
For tomorrow, I'll put on my makeup,
Cover up the spots and go on.
You'll then ask me if I'd like you to sleep next to me,
And I know you will bring so much peace,
But I am a war machine
Filled with bullets that only fire at me.
I have a tendency to form dependency;
I must refuse and choose the self-abuse,
Because I still believe that I must love myself.
But darling, if you see me drowning,
Jump in with a life jacket and sing me a lullaby,
Because if the space I occupy is overflowing,
The tears are leaking through the holes in my body,
Flooded with a supply
Of too much pain and sorrow.

A Love Letter to Karachi

You have fallen while others were on the rise,
You have lost mothers, daughters and wives,
And your fathers, sons and brothers have all sacrificed
For the beauty that you are, Karachi.
I have left you many times, only to return,
Although you constantly make my heart burn.
All I can do is complain like you're a friend,
But in the end,
You always make me smile for who you are, Karachi.
You have been painted red and wiped,
Your violence has been immensely hyped.
You have put fear into our souls,
But we still get out of our homes,
Because we are used to your mood swings, Karachi.

You have been corrupt and you have lied,
And plenty have died to keep you alive.
You're always on fire, ready to ignite,
But people travel to see you, the city of lights,
Because you are the queen of our hearts, Karachi.

Lahore may have its history,
Islamabad its nature,
But you in all glory,
Have it all, Karachi.
You hurt us over and over again,
We despise you over and over again,
But we're the clingy lovers who refuse to let you go.
We keep coming back for more,
You keep us on our tiptoes, Karachi.

Mass Murderer

You laugh when he says obnoxious things like,
"People have died in me," or
"I'm a desert, nothing grows here."
You admire his choice of words and metaphors,
But when a man tells you he has hosted funerals,
He is telling you he has murdered hearts.
When he tells you his body is dry,
Your tears will have no effect.
He's the airport that takes you to one destination,
And there's no return ticket.
He'll say you have hoarded him,
Docked your problems on him like he was your harbour,
But the truth is,
He broke all your ships.
There is no way out,
You live forever in him.
While he reincarnates,
And another girl laughs.
When he says,
"I'm night forever,"
Believe him.
He has sucked away sunshine before.

To Them

To the people who constantly tell me it's okay,
It's not.
Being heartbroken might be regular for you,
But I'm wretched to my core.
Like a vandalized car that had it's steering wheel stolen,
I'm standing here on wheels but I cannot move.

To the people who constantly tell me to smile,
I can't.
When the veins inside me are pumping only tears,
I'm hoping I can hold the weight and not drown.
You're asking me to row a boat and cross a river.

To the people who constantly pass me 'a little advice',
there's a reason why people are called big-mouthed and never big-eared.
Listening to things I cannot do is hard.

What a Wonderful Way to Live

The only kind of suffocation he knew,
He said was of love;
That is why he left his older relationships.
He said he was overwhelmed with affection,
Swimming in an entire ocean
As the only fish,
Sitting on the throne.
Being served like a king,
It felt claustrophobic, he said.
All this space in a person's heart to occupy,
No war to fight,
And all I could think was,
What a wonderful way to be out of breath.
What a wonderful way to drown.

A Late Realisation

I remember the way his eyes would roll up every time I kissed him,
and how that feeling gave me butterflies in my tummy,
flattering every inch of me while our skins rubbed against each other.

Later, I could only think,
Maybe his eyes would roll back
Hoping they could roll back to his mind,
Enough to find another face
To think of
While our lips would meet,
So that he,
Too,
Could feel as satisfied
As he made me feel.

Hurt Inspired

Maybe every tragedy is worth
Every art created,
For pain will never remain the same,
But the thought of it,
Stagnant.
Maybe no apology will heal
Published lines in a book.
Immortal feelings,
Sold,
A bestseller
Could be someone's death,
An autographed break-up,
An audience favourite.
Maybe every tragedy is worth
Every art created.

Foreign Territory

When the clothes came undone,
He could see the ruin that I was,
Like I had been conquered,
Colonised by strangers
Ripped from my roots to become
Somebody else's home.

It's the Thought That Counts

You talked about art created from pain.
Can I consider that you left
To assure my success?

Pun Intended

Life is an oxymoron,
Humorously depressing.
It tickles me in my throat,
When I laugh out curse words
At the emotional abuse you put me through.
Life is an oxymoron,
Painfully amusing.
When I tell people about what went wrong in my day,
I gather an audience, thirsty
To hear of a new misery.
Life is an oxymoron,
A beautiful lie,
Which wouldn't ever be believed
If it was spoken honestly.
Life is an oxymoron,
Happy alone.
You think I make no sense,
But I am sick of everyone else,
And that's the only truth.

Deceptive

You could package a bomb in a pretty box with a red ribbon
And it would still engulf the city in flames.
Your kind eyes were not a facade enough
For your cruel heart.

Tell Them

The next time they ask you what it feels like,
Tell them it feels like your body is slime,
Like your limbs were being pulled by strings,
But even your puppeteer is tired.

Tell them it feels like
You're a watercolour painting
A child was working on and got angry in the middle.
All the colours are everywhere.

Tell them it feels like
You were lying in the middle of the road,
And a tanker toppled over you.
Your body is squeezed under the weight of a vehicle.

Tell them
It's like choking on peanuts or kiwis or sesame

Tell them it feels like
Swinging,
And being swung so high up,
You never come back.

Tell them it's like
There's a balloon flying really high in the sky,
And you blew into it,
All the air in your lungs.

Tell them it's like
Being asked to walk on a tightrope,
And you are afraid of heights.
Tell them it's like
You're being rung from the afterlife,
Like death wants to speak to you
And call you home.
You're trying to disconnect the cable wires,
But there are a hundred of them connected to one phone,
And you are certain the one you cut
Will trigger a bomb,
And kill with you everybody else you love.

Tell them
It's like being charged with murder
And being sentenced to life.
For twenty minutes,
You're surrounded by protestors who demand your blood,
But you aren't guilty of the crime.
Tell them it's like
Going back into the womb
Of a mother who doesn't want you to survive.
There's little space and a lot of darkness

Like being buried alive,
In a backyard of a friend who has a party going on.
Your wails

Are silence.

A Lyrical Affair

Glide your fingers over me like I am a piano,
Pull my hair like you're plucking guitar strings.
Caress my skin and cause friction
Like I'm a violin and you're an arco.
Blow warm air into my mouth; I'm a flute,
Let our bodies create the chorus.
Let our throats sing the song of lust,
Let the bed witness a concert.

When A Boy Becomes A Man

0: The louder I wail, the softer her cradle,
Her arms are my crib and her eyes my musical mobile.

2: He yells at her, "Why is there only a birthday cake?"
Didn't he tell her twice he'd be calling over friends?
Apologies made, she ruffles my hair, arches her back, and returns to the kitchen.

6: She's drenched like a mop as she picks me up from school.
Sun or rain, she still had to clean up the mess.
Emergency contact, vomit stained shorts, I've been sick.
Blue, bruised neck; has she too been ill?

8: Man and wife, beat, repeat, she cries defeat.
Memorise it; like you hold the bible,
Whether or not you understand it.
Marriage is the edge of a knife,
I draw a heart with her blood when he's not looking,
Take it to my tongue and taste it.

10: I pull her hair; girls like to be teased,
Scrunched face like a wet cloth being squeezed.
Her face says differently, she's not pleased.

12: I bend down to check the colour of her panties,
"Told you they're pink," coughed up pennies, won the bet.
Trespassed into a private space, I had no invite,
It was never a party anyway

18: She said she needed a friend,
But she was home alone.
Exert power, 'NO' is not the word of God.

Did she look like she had fun?
Eyes like a corpse, moving limbs like she was dancing,
Her struggling breath becoming her song,
Pale like snow-white, damsel in distress.
I wore my shining armour
Oh yeah, she looked like she is lucky a man like me chose her.

~~Hero~~ Zero

I wish your parents had allowed you to shed tears,
So, you wouldn't fear your masculinity
And wear it like a cape,
Believing that your super power
Was the ability to make her cry.

Rapacious

I held onto you in the hope that maybe one day I'd be able to see a part of you that has learned to accommodate from his mother, who silently kept you inside her body, let you make it your home, and hoard the space. Often violently, you kicked and brought her pain. Yet she remained silent, like she had been taught to make space for the men in her life. She made space for her little, rapacious boy. You were born weighing ten pounds straight, and all you remember is making a woman scream and wail. You thought that was praise thrown at the sight of you. How can you now walk into someone's life and not leave without them crying and wailing for you? Oh, you say you were born that way.

Cliche

"It's not you, it's me."
Believe him the next time he tells you it's his fault
For not loving you.
He was the empty vase
You filled with flowers,
And no matter how many tears you pour,
You cannot make a garden grow
In drought.

Domestic Disaster

You had become a volcano,
Eruptable with a single touch.
So, we tiptoed around the house,
Afraid to wake you up.
Your screams silenced us,
And isn't it crazy
How opposites attract?
The mute kept
Circling around,
The loud,
Appeasing, pleasing
The unpleasant,
Till there was no doubt
There was only one ruler abode:
Anger.

After the First Time

After the first kiss, you don't think you can feel this high again. The kind of high that makes you feel vulnerable, like knots in your gut, twisting. The butterflies are on drugs, soaring, not getting enough space in your little stomach to fly. Endorphins racing with no finish line. You are afraid of heights, but you tell yourself this is the last time you'll climb up so far. You will fall, not hard enough to die, but to break a few limbs or two; enough to carry a crutch and limp through the next phases of a relationship you are never sure will last, that you will hope lasts, even if it means you have to hop on one leg.

After the first time you sleep in a lover's bed, you'll sneak into his bathroom, stare at yourself in the mirror and clean it, hoping to remove the spots that appear over your skin like constellations he traces, saying he has found his favourite. He'll name it 'the quantum leap.' You'll realise the marks are not stains, but your own imperfect reflection. You'll make your way back to the bedroom, admire the silhouette that rises up and down as he breathes, and meditate, fixated on the rhythm of the movement of his chest. You'll note it down; you have found the God you can worship.

After the first time you travel with a partner, you'll find a map together that shows all the possible routes to your heart. You'll swear you have never been found that easily, convinced that you were lost, dug deep inside like a treasure field, but your lover is a gold miner. You will hang bags on your shoulders that carry your stories that weigh a ton. You will carve memories with your fingertips on the sandy shores. You will yell forever from the mountain tops, hoping your voice reaches the heaven reserving a spot for the two of you.

Nothing will ever seem the same way for the second or third time. You'll leave seconds of déjà vu on the lips of others who'll visit your once abandoned home. You will forget the first pillow you laid your head on, and learn to adjust into sunk-in dents made by other strangers who've been there before. You'll become a lodger, with your shoulders weighed down when you visit another country, with another voice who yells along with yours, and you'll stop believing in the heavens. The world will be flat, you will no longer dare to play hide and seek, afraid he'll hide so well that he'll never be discovered. You will never climb high enough, or see a man as more than a man when you look into his eyes or hope for eternity, when you can only see as far as your sight goes. You'll become practical, selfish, stronger and will start to look inside your own skin, stitching the layers where wounds have cut deep. You will drop your binoculars and pick up a microscope, no more looking into the future but closely at the present, reading in between the lines better than ever before.

You'll believe repetition will decrease the intensity of pain, but the only thing that will feel worse will be the second, third, fourth heartbreak. You'll be surprised at how much heart you still have left. When more of it is ripped out of your chest, you just don't run out of enough beats to steal away. No matter how many times "I don't love you," rings in your ears, the sound will be new. You've been educated before; read over and over on how to not be this weak, but you will still crumble like ice cream in scorching heat. Standing in front of the dragon that's blowing out fire burning you, you'll have no hero to call out for, no shield to protect you, and, once again, you'll be left bare naked out on the street, in your home, or at another train station. When will you run out of destinations to be thrown to, to start over, to feel all the new emotions you can feel, and then be crushed and destroyed, yet again?

Ordinary Cold March

i. Not a sign of spring; this motherfucking cold is biting me down
    my ass, my feet, and my toes, the numbness driving rants to be
    spat out.

No sunshine, grey clouds, rain and gloomy London days where men
embrace you in their arms day and night and caress you. There isn't an
escape from what you have been told is love.

Standing tall and strong, rooted like the trees, you are to be admired by
passers-by who sit under your shade and never bother to see if you've been
watered.

Without colour on your face, you look the same; fragile but you're no
cutting-edge woman, just too safe.

Emotions always out of control, like leaves that go haywire when the wind
blows, the pout of your lips makes no man lose control. You forget your
function in a world of purpose.

What did you want to be when you grew up? I mean, more than a mother
or somebody's wife. A little more exciting, perhaps the slutty mistress of
the next-door neighbour?

Are you going to tell me you had a dream that made you stand on your
feet instead of your knees? Did you say you read and want to create a
string of words that make people see you as one of them, or perhaps just
a human being?

You aspire more than you can inspire, and a fire that strong is a waste of
wood, so burn down the desire to be anything more than a body that can
bleed, birth, and survive,

You were never the warrior, but the slave that was won post war, imprisoned and kept to clean the enclave of those who'd rule and fuck, and make you pretend that it was pleasure.

Why did you expect another year to be another weather, when March has always been a betrayal to worshippers of the flowers who pray for them to bloom?

Minutes, days, months, rapid ticks on the clocks and trails of ants on the ground know when there is danger, and change their route towards their homes.

Time for you stands restrained, handcuffed and regulated. You are governed by the larger footprints left over mud, there is nowhere else you'd rather sink when comfort has become your master.

ii. Ordinary woman, it never really ends,
Ordinary woman, go and plead forgiveness,
Ordinary woman, there isn't any use of making amends,
Ordinary woman, wish upon stars,
Ordinary woman, they aren't yours to wish upon,
Ordinary woman, when will you live?
Ordinary woman, you were not allowed to live,
Ordinary woman, you stay pure and never misbehave,
Ordinary woman, you have sinned.
You keep breathing despite everything.
Ordinary woman,
You need to smile more.

Myths

I was taught from a young age,
That men are vampires,
Who will blow away candles,
Suck away your happiness,
Having faith that the night is on their side.
And, without sight,
Your hands will be tied, disadvantaged.
But you are a bat,
Consummated in the dark.
You can distinguish a touch,
You can navigate anywhere,
And lead yourself to the light.
The truth is, you have always existed,
And the fear of them
Has just been a myth.

No Surplus

There is only so much you can give someone,
There is only so much water a sea can hold before it floods an entire city.
I know you think you are responsible for unburdening everyone of their worries,
And you love helping spread smiles all around you,
But nobody sees the process of creating happiness for others.
You're choking your own brightness,
Distributing enough light so the neighbourhood can remain lit.
You're not the damn sun;
Some days you do not want to rise,
And if you keep giving away your scented candles,
You'll be left with darkness,
And no fuel to create fire.

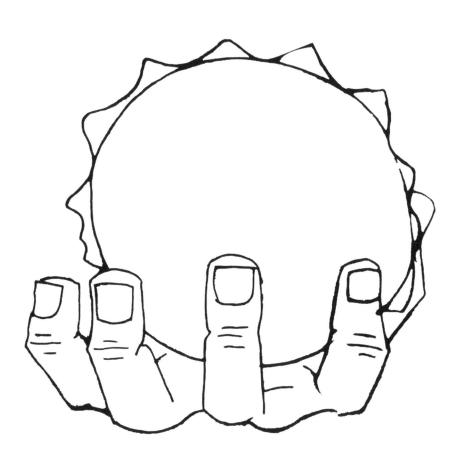

Sunday Brunch

There you are, at the family gathering, sitting in a corner,
Wearing crème and camouflaging with the vanilla sofa,
But your reputation precedes you.
You anxiously recite numbers,
The countdown till somebody asks you what's on your mind.
You pray that you can bite your tongue,
Blood will taste less bitter
Than your thoughts that can roll like bowling balls
Towards trembling relatives,
Who swear
The words you carry,
Weigh a ton more than your body.
You can't bring discomfort to the comfortable,
The outside to those who remain glued inside.

An aunt approaches, she can smell the urge in you to escape.
Tonight you'll be her prey,
And she will blame you for getting sick,
When you'll be the one who'll word vomit.
She makes a comment then about you ageing,
Marriage, but marriage with a Sunni guy,
Marriage with a man at least five years older,
Marriage with a Pakistani,
Marriage with a man who can knock some sense into this feminist
nonsense,
Marriage with an entire family,
Marriage executed grandiosely,
Marriage decided by elders.
She declares the type of guy you need to end up with,
And adds an emotional note about how your grandma may die,

So you must make this soon.
Go to Europe for your honeymoon,
Bring a bundle of joy who can wail his lungs out,
Be passed around from arm to arm,
Each arm deciding his faith, name and virtue,
Then have you be left alone
To deal with it.

You'll try to swallow your dinner quietly,
But you don't take her attempts to annoy you lightly.
She'll then ask you
To join them to pray,
And you'll say,
"I can't."
She'll say, "What a shame,
You'll burn in flames."
When you go to hell,
Remember how I yelled,
"You do nothing but disobey!"
You'll say, "I'm on my period,"
And everyone around will gasp
And grasp their hearts.
For how could you say out loud,
The biological process of your body,
Amongst a crowd that includes some males,
Who they all assume are so innocent,
That they accept their wives not having sex,

Once a week in a month
That has nothing to do with the woman's choice
And their own masculinity,
But to speak of what everyone knows is still considered taboo.
You have stunned and turned the humans to statues.

Every month, when you meet faces you've seen growing up that have
changed,
You'll realize nothing else has,
And more devastating than that is,
That they do not want to.
Frozen in the ice age,
Every event ends in a rampage,
As soon as you decide to be yourself.

Prepared For the Worst

I remember the stalkers, the pretend phone calls, keys ready in hand and
a very strong heartbeat.
You could no longer be a female on the street,
You were never a person walking, making her way to the supermarket to
buy some eggs.
But just a pair of breasts,
Like items scanned at the counter.
Different nationalities, but harassment has no race,
They wouldn't remember your face
Or address you with a name,
But you'd remember the eyes,
Feel the shame
For having visited dirty minds
Were you fourteen when your body started changing?
You can't recall,
But ask your uncle - he'll tell you all
About how the colour of your first bra was blue,
And when your mother found your blood-stained underwear
And smiled.
You cried,
Breaking out of denial, it was true.
You were growing up,
You never wanted to.

Bloom

Maybe he was a flower.
He only started blooming,
When my tears started pouring down.

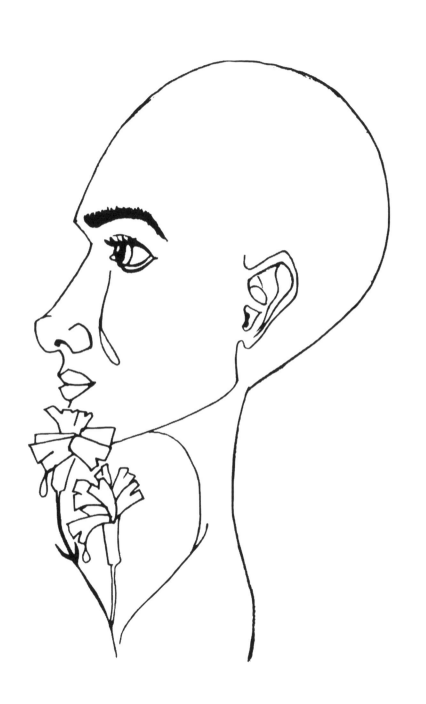

Artists

We artists are egoistic arseholes
Who think the world works exactly as we know.
We're cynical, satirical and pretty damn mean,
Except our irony works a lot better than your words,
So you believe when we claim our intellectuality,
When we mind fuck your questions
And we ruin your make belief,
We let you break our hearts purposely,
Immortalise you into our muse.
We usually do choose
To be pathetically miserable.

But we artists, don't want you to know,
These emotions tend to grow,
When we put our organs on our sleeves.
So, I'll pretend that I can debate
And I will make you lose,
By saying a super interesting thing,
A made-up theory thrown into your face.
"She's so damn smart," is all I really want to hear.

Now ask me what love is
And watch me get tongue tied,
For it's the only thing I cannot explain,
A lesson I couldn't learn.
The first time, I couldn't say "No", when my mother said,
"If your friends jumped off a cliff, would you follow?"
I wanted to fall into the abyss
That nobody comes out from the same.
They all held me in their arms like musical instruments to be played,
Gliding their fingers over me like pianists

Like magicians who'd received their magic lamps.
I was rubbed, pleased, never objected,
But could never give whatever was expected,
From the one to
The other, not enough.
Too loud, too angry, too sad, too happy,
The writer was broken down into categories.

Then love would call off the celebrations,
Migrate off to another host,
Leaving you with the ghost
Of fights, lies, the rebound guys.
And you'd drink to make yourself feel whole,
But darling, don't you know,
Every after party,
Ring the same songs,
And shower pieces of confetti shaped into broken hearts.
I collect you like I'm collecting the sea
Of plenty of fish,
And I'm going to boast because I've gotten pretty rich.

"What is love?" They'll ask me,
And I'll shiver to my bones,
For the question that makes me stutter,
Makes me blabber
A bunch of names.
God and the devil reside in the same place;
Forget it then, end him like a bad story,
A faulty character. Think of it as a plot twist,
Crunched paper balls in rubbish bins are reaching the top
Of failed beginnings, missed chapters.

What is love?
A painful sentence that doesn't end with a full stop.

Autocorrect

I wish I could autocorrect life,
So every time someone is about to say something horrible, I can just auto-
correct them,
Like people making fun of me being overweight.
Our conversations would just sound like: "Have you gained some more
beauty?"
I'm sick and tired of hearing negative comments,
Like it's your duty
To preach to me about what you think of my body.

I want to become a sea, and erase
Words that shouldn't be in place,
So nobody has to feel pain
That bashes at their certainty.
Someone the other day, watched a performance by me
And said,
"You were great!"
"But dude, you almost covered the entire stage!"
From then on, I could never watch that video
Without cringing about how I look less human and more like mould.

If I could autocorrect, your mouth would only speak about peace,
So when you tell me it's so funny that the British opted for Brexit,
Your fist can bump your throat and correct you,
So instead you can say, "It's so sad what the world is becoming."

If I could autocorrect,
Every time a woman tells me she's not a feminist,
Her own words could kick her in her arse,
Just like she's stabbing us in the back,
And sound more like,
"I hate women who keep hating on women!"

If I could autocorrect,
I would write the truth,
So whenever my fingers press the keys
They could freeze
Like a paralysis has taken over me,
And contemplate the lie
They're about to leak.
So, instead of typing, 'I'm fine,'
I could really explain
The emotions tumbling inside me,
Like dirty laundry
In a washing machine,
And this time you can hear
"I really need you, can you stay a little longer?"

If I could autocorrect,
I'd go back to my past
And give you the hate you deserve and the love you did not,
Because wounds that are cut,
Never really shut,
And now they leak of mistakes,
So when you lay your head

On my chest and confessed,
And asked me if I felt the same,
My words should have shook my bones,
So I could say, "Gross, I've always thought of you as a friend!"
And that would be the end.

If I could autocorrect,
Every time a man walked passed by me
And whispered, "Hot," and licked his lips
Or slapped my hips,
He could just come up and say, "Hello,"
Because, who knows? Maybe that conversation starter
Would be considered more humane,
And I'd actually speak to you?

If I could autocorrect
A friend,
Maybe I would've slept that night
When he sent me a screenshot of my ex- at a party
And laughed, "Do you want to see how happy he looks?"
I wished he had a filter which wouldn't allow him to type
Without thinking.
He could've said, "Hey, I know you checked his Facebook. I'm here for you."

If I could autocorrect myself,
I would replace every time I said "Yes"

With "No."
And perhaps I'd be taller today,
To have statements made by strangers
Pass by me
Like shooting stars
You hear about,
But hardly get to see.
And it would not matter
That I don't have this technology
Instilled in me.
But the truth is,
I autocorrect people around me continuously.
They say I get very angry sometimes,
And I agree,
Because there's a glitch in your vocabulary.
So, wherever you search for your words,
They just roll at me like balls of fire,
Meant to burn.
And all I ever hear,
Is that, "Dear,
You're not worth it."

Aim, shoot, break

My heart is
A dart board,
And I have left the buttons of my shirt open.

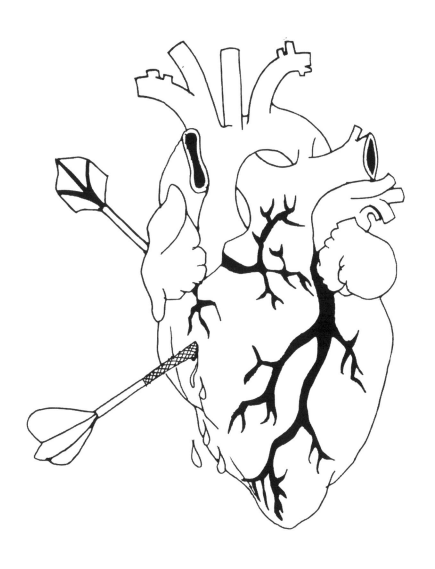

Maybe

Maybe this isn't the destination. Maybe where you are right now is the transit. That doesn't mean you aren't travelling, you can't be a rock, stuck in a moment. You need to be sand, swept away and landed wherever the wind takes you. Maybe you're a nomad with no home. And maybe that's good; maybe you'll never be homeless, and that is something to be happy about. Maybe aeroplanes were created for people who fall in love in different time zones, those who buy smiles at the duty-free shops so they can present their best ones once they arrive. Maybe all the struggle is worth it; like a bug caught in a spider's web, release will not come easily, but the fight is necessary. Maybe we're flowers and need to pass through our bloom and our fall. But wherever we may be, parts of us will drift away to a new place and help us regrow all over again. Maybe we'll be a new colour this time, maybe we'll hope we can still smell the same.

An Ode to My Retainer

Only before bed time,
I accept my imperfections
When the makeup peels off,
And my pores are exposed,
I am from head to toe myself.
I pick you up from the bathroom shelf,
And place you between my jaws,
And deep in my mouth,
You know of all the lies I have told
Like, "I definitely do not wear you anymore",
Like "I am confident about the way I look."
A taste of awkward teenage years,
And still miserably trying to look like something one can accept,
Except the only gap that increases
Is not in the middle of my thighs,
But the middle of my teeth.
I drape myself in a loose tee,
And dream about a time
I can breathe in a pair of skinny jeans,
The skin between my legs not chaffed
From walking too far,
And when I can laugh
Without tracing my tongue over the hole
That smiles back at you,
Displaying my incompleteness.
Only before bed time,
I confess,
I am struggling to be a whole,
I'm still looking for parts of me to grow.

Note from Author

Hi reader,

I hope that you enjoyed this read. I hope you were able to relate and realise that you are not alone in feeling a lot of things that you do feel. I also wish that it helped you feel more empowered and this helps you express, and start conversations about things that matter to you and affect the lives of people around you.

It took a lot to complete this book. Months of planning, compiling and a whole lot of editing to be able to provide something for you to hold in your hands. It would never have been completed without the following people: my parents, my sisters (Sarah and Rabia), my best friends (Zoha, Mariam and Aimen), my UK support system (Samad, Lindsey, Lizi and Ivana), my editor Simon Richardson and the incredibly talented illustrator of this book, Aaiza Alam.

Thank you to all the above mentioned and anybody else I met along this journey who motivated me and supported my endeavour. Especially the hosts of all the poetry events I attended who let me take over their stages for a couple of minutes to share my story.

This has been my biggest achievement to date but will not be the biggest. Follow my Instagram and Twitter to keep up to date with my new goals I have yet to reach.

Instagram: @Writeroholic
Twitter: @AnnumSalman

Much love,

Annum Salman

About Author

Annum Salman left the PR world in Pakistan to travel to England for an MA in Creative Writing at the University of Surrey. She writes about family, love, her experiences as a woman and a minority. As a spoken word poet she has had successful performances at the 1000 Monkeys, Write Out Loud, Surrey's New Writers Festival and feature shows at Dorking is Talking, and That's What She Said in Shoreditch. She has also performed in Malaysia as well as in Karachi and Lahore- having been a finalist from Karachi for the Pakistan Poetry Slam in Lahore. When not writing, she is found painting in her scarce alone time or hanging out with her newly adult friends and laughing about the ironies of life. Whatever she may do and wherever she may end up, she will always remain a storyteller.

About The Illustrator

Aaiza Alam is a Pakistani illustrator who studied Fine Arts from IVSAA, Karachi (2010) and Fashion Communication from CSM, London (2014). Born and raised in Karachi, Alam has been involved in the Pakistani creative industry since 2011, where she has branched out from radio, print magazine, event management, television and more providing her an outlet for her creative energy. Experimenting with different mediums, Alam does not limit herself to visuals but is also a voice over artist since 2013, lending her voice not just to commercials but documentaries and children's animations. In pursuit of understanding the power of expression, Alam also received training as an art therapy practitioner under NOWPDP (2013) where she got an opportunity to work pro bono for children with disabilities. Currently she is working as a content writer for PH Solutions – an Influencer Management, Strategic Brand Management & Public Relations company in Pakistan.

Printed in Great Britain
by Amazon